On the Wings of the Moon

Anja J.

To all the girls
Who carry hurricanes within their souls

"The moon is friend for the lonesome to talk to."

Carl Sandburg

CONTENTS

WAXING CRESCENT
MOON

Creative hand

What are our lives
If not poems
Written and erased
By the creative hand
Of life

Moments

My body is made out of moments
Which shaped me
Carving themselves
Deeply into my chest
Memories are my bricks
My skin is parchment
On which Destiny writes all over
People leave their ink on me
Sometimes spilling it

Not enough

I have learned to crawl
Because the world
Invited me to explore it
I have learned to walk
Because my heart
Ached to climb mountains
I have learned to run
Because my feet
Were too excited
Then I learned to fly
Because the ground
Wasn't enough anymore

Adventures

My childhood
Was a careless climb
To high mountains
And swimming
In the deep blue ocean
With no fear
Because I knew
You would always be there
To give me a hand
So even jumping across
Sharp rocks
Seemed like an adventure
Even when I got cut
I knew there was
No reason to panic
Not because it didn't hurt
But because you showed me
That sometimes
Life will make you bleed
But you will be there
To tend to the wounds
And we will continue
Our adventure
Never looking back

Burning on the inside

Sun is dancing
All over my
Closed eyelids
It's inviting me
To take a leap
Back to the past
Go to the times
When I rode
My old red bike
On the dirt road
Through the green
Corn fields
When sunflowers
Followed me with
Their dark eyes
And I felt protected
By their warm
Watchful attention
When air felt so hot
That just existing
Outside on the sun
Felt like swimming
In a pool of hot
Invisible steam
When the ground
Was burning
But the grass was fresh
And its touch was
 A gentle caress

Of the summer
When nothing
Was burning
On the inside
And the only thing
I thought about
Was the next bike ride

Nostalgia

Nostalgia feels
Like gentle touch
Of a mother's hand
Caressing your hair
On a sunny day
And like a punch in the gut
By the big strong man
At the crowded bar
In the late hours of the night
It smells sweetly
Of cookies and ginger
Until you feel the staleness
Of beer and alcohol
On its breath
You forgive nostalgia
Its destructive touch
Because it brings you
Sugar, spice and everything nice
But you know the high
Won't last forever
You will need another dose
Another trip
Back to the past
It's a vicious circle
That never ends
Until you realize
Memories are just another
Type of ecstasy

Haven

Looking at
The hard life
You, my dearest grandma
Had to endure,
I admire you
With every fiber of my being
No other person
Would have that much
Strength
To work and love
With such ferocity
That the earth shakes
When it feels your presence
You are made
Out of earth and clay
Shaped by rough winds
And ice rains
But your core
Is a warm fireplace
Where the souls
Of people you love live
Enveloped in
Your soft embers
Knowing
That for them
There is no safer
Haven

Possibilities

Swimming
In the unknown
Makes you think
There are sharks
Circling around you
So you wait for
Their sharp bite
Unaware of
The colorful
Kingdom of
Possibilities
That awaits
You in
Your next dive

Safe place

If I could take your heart
And keep it in mine
I would be happiest
Because then I would know
You would always
Be happy and safe
But you too deserve
To feel all the emotions
So be free
Experience the world
And yet know
That my heart
Will always be there
As a home for you
A safe place
Where no harm
Can happen

Paint

Sometimes I paint
With a brush
Sometimes I paint
With words
The most important
Thing is
That my color
Is in both cases
Love

Summer night

Scent of a warm
Summer night
Smells undoubtedly
Like the long walks
Under the stars
Emerging from depths
Of my childhood
My senses tremble
With memories unleashed
And I swim back in time

Escape

My memories are warm
Golden from the sun
With so many scents
Mixing and twirling inside
My mind
I yearn to melt away
My whole being inside them
If only for a moment
To escape the present time

Time travel

A strange scent
Catches my senses
I am certain
I have felt it once before
An unknown memory
Keeps knocking
On my mind
Remember me! Come back!
That moment is buried deep
In my consciousness
Under so many layers of thoughts
Thick and hard paths
Of my mind
I want to peel each
And every one of them
Break them one by one
Open that door
And find myself
In that unfamiliar happy place
From my past
That I have grown to love
So dearly
How can they say
Time travel is not possible
When past flirts with me
So ferociously

To my sister

You are a dance
Of swords and flowers
An eternal fight
Between love and fire

Nymph

Summer showers
When I was a child
Smelled undoubtedly
Of danger
The sepia skies
The blue thunders
The passionate wind
They all invited me to dance
I was in danger
Of being more free
Of surrendering myself
To the waves of Imagination
And dance around
Jumping in puddles
Barefoot and with
Rose cheeks
Just like a nymph
Rejoicing in nature

Ecstasy

I am dependant on
That sweet, terrible feeling
That perfect point
Between the giddiness
Provoked by
My happiest memories
And despair
Because they are gone
Never to return again
Those two mixed
Together
Are my elixir and my poison
My ecstasy

Colors

I paint the world around me
With every color of my soul
So the world and everyone in it
Become my masterpiece

WAXING GIBBOUS MOON

Change

Surrender
To the waves of change
They will take you
To new worlds
You carry home
Within your soul
Not within places
And things
That only hold you back

Possibilities

Swimming
In the unknown
Makes you think
There are sharks
Circling around you
So you wait for
Their sharp bite
Unaware of
The colorful
Kingdom of
Possibilities
That awaits
You in
Your next dive

Thrilling

Jumping
Into the sea of change
Can be scary
But the delight of a
New adventure
Is even more thrilling
Than fear

Flirting

The wind flirts with me
Through the leaves
Of the trees
It invites me
To be free
Awaken the blood
Of my brave
Ancestresses
Roam the prairies
Run with the stars

Night dance

The night is dancing
Around my body
Seducing it slowly
With its enchanting
Rhythm of ease
Droplets of moonlight
Drip all over my skin
I forget my fear
And surrender it
To the fields of dark
I am bathed whole
In the gentle hands
Of the darkness
Its melody sways me
And releases my joy
Diamonds sparkle
All over the sky
I long for their love
It's the reason
I dance with the Night
I release my spirit
So one day
I can rise
High above the fields
And touch them
The way they touched me

Wandering

Some people
Love to wander
Because of the freedom
It gives them
To not be attached
Some people
Are afraid to wander
Because the freedom
Of too many opportunities
Is too hard to handle
But we are all nomads
In our lives
We all wander
Feel lost at times
Yes it is scary
Yes it is uncertain
But when life gives you
A blank page
Whether to write
Paint or destroy it
Seize the opportunity
Create art
Create life

Living

Dancing to the soft rhythm
Of my mind and soul
Stripping and remaining nude
Exposes my delicate parts
But that's how poems are born

I never ask for silence

Words dance their
Feral rhythm around me
Attacking me sometimes
Stabbing me with
Their dangerous truths
There are times
They kidnap my mind
And keep it prisoner
For days with no end
But the few moments
When they pour into me
Unspeakable beauty
I see the world's
Endless magnificence
That is the reason
I never ask for silence

Search

I search for all
The beautiful words

Let them come to me
Let them enchant me
With their sharpness
Surrendering to their magic
They are a gateway
To another dimension
I find pure beauty
Painless state of freedom
Explosive moment of ecstasy
I do not fear words
Though they can cut me
And bruise me and hurt me
It is a sweet sorrow
To find the perfect one

Night is my lover

Night is my lover

Every evening I run
Losing my breath
Filling my lungs with its wonder
Straights into its arms
It envelops me whole in its embrace
And whispers gently
You are marvelous
You are bliss

Temptress

Dearest Moon
You flirty temptress
You have enchanted me
With your silky magic
Seduced my body
With your call of wild
And I have become
One of your slaves
Ever looking for
Your doting touch
In shadow coloured
Nights

Let's run with the stars

Let's run with the stars
Let's unleash our inner dark
Surrender to the
Blackest of black
And find beauty
In that feeling
Of the complete lack of control
Aren't you curious to know
What it feels like
To let go of your hopes and fears
And dive into the unknown
Head first
When you might easily crash
Let's give permission
To the stars to guide us
Far away from our normal selves
And into new worlds
Where inhibitions don't exist
And our souls are made
Out of pure energy of
Freedom

Freedom

I love it when
I let go of everything
Let my storms loose
On everything around me
Am I ever more myself
Than when my rain
Engulfs the world
Oh it feels so good
To be able to
Run with the Moon
This is what I needed
Freedom

Wild Beauty

It was the breath of a monsoon
That made you come to life
And it was the moon dust
That built your body
You were created
To be a force of nature
To bring tide to the ocean
And winds to the storms
The earthquakes of your love
Shatter your entire being
But bits of you regenerate
When exposed to moonlight
Though people know
You could electrify their soul
And leave them in pieces
They cannot resist loving you
The tornado of you
Pulls them in your magic
And they are frozen forever
In the lake of wild beauty

Rejoice in your wildness

You were born
Out of hurricane's breath
Your soul was bathed
In sudden summer showers
Your body was built
Out of meteorite rocks
Your whole existence
Is made out of wild
So run free with
The other beasts
That is where
You truly belong

Wild summer night

Let's open the window
And let in the heat
Of a wild summer night
Let's run away together
With bare feet
Dancing on the grass
Let us be young
Just a little bit more
A little bit longer
A little bit crazier
Unleash the wildness
From our cores
There is no tomorrow
Let's run and dance
Naked and free
And never look behind
Oh please let's run away
Out of my mind

FULL MOON

Tragedy

Tragedy has
A malicious way to
Sneak into your life
You don't see it coming
Until it is already there
Painting your entire world
In shades of black
Even if you try
To scrape away the paint
All you are left with
Are bloody fingertips

Fishing net

In moments of panic
I close my eyes
I clog my ears
And scream on the inside
This isn't happening!
This isn't happening!
This isn't happening!
But deep down
 I know you can't stop
A flood
With a fishing net

Remembered

You were a shining light
In our darkness
Our figure of speech
Our pillar of life
You were a comet that
Enlightened the sky
Passing too fast
You exploded with colors
You were a grain of sand
In the midst of storms
Twisting and twirling
Carried by the rain
Always to be remembered
Never to be caught

Missing

When you left
The problem wasn't
That I would miss you
The problem was
That I would miss you
Forever

Cracks

I can't remember
The last time we spoke
On the phone
It must have been ages ago
When you were still well
And your voice was
Its usual cheerful self
Or maybe it was when you have
Already started wilting
So I stopped calling
Speaking to you only in person
Because I feared
That it the distance and rumor
Of a phone line
Would showcase
The cracks in your voice
That I was so desperately
Trying to ignore

Our choice

Why do things happen
I guess that is
An unanswerable question
Maybe we all have to
Come to this strange place we call Earth
So that we could learn certain things
And it's our souls
Who choose the lessons in advance
Before we are born
We make a deal with everyone
Whom we will meet during our lifetime
And we say
You will teach me this
And I will teach you that
It is somehow easier to believe
That our suffering
Was our own choice
Because of a greater purpose
Not an accident of the Universe

Theft

It's strange how
Certain events
Make such an impression
That they delete
All the future events
From your head
That is the reason
I don't remember many
Moments from my life
In the months
After you died
Your departure
Stole them from me

Anxiety

Its grip is strong
Yet ticklish
It might feel
Like it is
Caressing me
Lovingly
But in reality
It is poking
My innocent flesh
With its ugly claws

Panic

It rises from my toes
All the way to my mind
Crushing my chest
With its cruel fist
Pieces of me
Get lost every time
I don't see the way out
So I plunge to the bottom
Because from there
The only way is up

Sadness

Sadness is my blue mother
Her train sparkles with tears
She caresses my face
With a gentle hand
Enveloping me in her cloak
She puts me to sleep
Among the other stars
Singing the known lullaby
Of far away roads
And endless transformations
I run away from her
Hiding in the bare mountains
But not for too long
Her soothing embrace
Summons me too strongly
So I let go of myself
Unable to move forward

Endless pit

Depression feels
Like an endless pit
Of dirt and slime
That constantly
Pulls you down
You fight for breath
With your weak hands
Occasionally clawing
The walls of the dark
But the soft mud
Gets in everywhere
It fills your lungs
It embraces your arms
It caresses your back
Until it comes
To your eyes
It closes your eyelids
So you couldn't see
That there is a way out
So you stay there
For long time
Unaware of the light

Move mountains

Sometimes I can
Move mountains
With a flick of my thought
And sometimes even mountains
Can't move me
From that place of darkness
I have grown to know
So personally

Two close friends

When Depression
And Anxiety
Become your
Two closest friends
And talk to you
Almost constantly
For a long time
It is easy to forget
Those good times
When they were
Absent from your life

Tired

That feeling of
Infinite fatigue
Has been consuming
My body
For a while now
If I could feel
Any emotion
It would scare me
That it is holding me
Prisoner
And doesn't seem
To have any inclination
To take off
Its slimy hands
From my soft heart

Numb

What I fear the most
Is being so numb
That even words
Don't visit my mind anymore
To create new worlds
Inside my head
Instead there is nothing
But darkness
Even the stars
Are gone

Stone

A stone lies in my chest
It pushes all other emotions down
It drags me to the bottomless pit
As I struggle to carve words on it
I push it, and nothing seems to work
My fingertips bleed from trying to lift
When finally my tears wet the stone
Bathing it in its fruitless attempts
I see my own reflection in it

Cracked vase

Sometimes I feel that
Tragedy has destroyed me
Beyond repair
That no matter what I do
No matter how much love
I have to give
I will never be whole again
Even if you gather
All my broken pieces
I will forever remain
That cracked old vase
Glued together clumsily
Ever standing
But unable to
Nourish flowers ever again

Lack

I am not afraid
Of being overwhelmed
By emotions
I am afraid of
Not feeling anything
At all

Let me talk

They never let me
Talk about you anymore
Your existence has become
A taboo
A secret that no one
Seems to want to find out
A pink elephant in the room
Beautiful, lively, happy
But clumsy
Reminding us of just how
Fragile we are
Why don't they ask me
What you thought
About world politics
How you dressed
What was the color
Of your laugh
It's not a secret that you
Have existed
It's not a secret
Everyone suffered when you left
So why am I not allowed
To talk about you anymore
Why can't I express my happiness
About your existence
When memories
Are the only thing
I have from you

Explosion

The problem when
You have no one to talk to
Is that your whole insides
Are bubbling with need
To get out
And you feel speechless
At the same time
As if someone put
A lid on your mouth
So nothing could get out
You feel
An explosion coming
And you know
You can't stop it

Pillage the world

I finally understand
Why storms exist
Why monsoons destroy
Entire worlds sometimes
It is the rage of
Mother Earth

No, don't ever give me
The power of the storms
Because when I think
About how you died
I want to raise thunder
And earthquakes
Pillage this world
Destroy every beautiful thing
Because I will never understand
Why did it have to
Happen like that

Raging

I sometimes feel
Less like a person
And more like a storm
Raging at the world

Abusive relationship

Anger
Has been my companion
For too long
I sometimes feel
That without it
I wouldn't know
How to function properly
But it is like that
Painfully handsome
Boyfriend
Who wakes up fire
In your core
But cheats and lies
Hurts you all the time
So why do I remain
In this abusive relationship

Dirt

Why am I unable to cry
When crying
Are just my clouds
Releasing their rain
And washing away
The dirt
Of my thoughts

Wildness lost

When did I lose
My wildness
Maybe it was among
The demands of life
That became overwhelming
I couldn't be brave anymore
So I settled with being small
Now I feel like a shaky
Scared animal
Afraid to not only
Leave its nest
But to even look at the sky

WANING GIBBOUS MOON

Let go

Thunder is the sound
Of my insides screaming
You need to let go
So just like the heavy
Gray clouds announcing
Chaos and storms
My eyes fill with tears
My breath becomes wind
And I release the wild pain
That cuts right through me
Into the world
As the thirsty ground feeds
On the salt of my tears
And my soul is bathed
In purifying pool of rain
I realize the sky isn't
Dark any longer
Its blue color is the shade
Of a new beginning

Choose

Maybe I just need to cry
To let the emotions out
Not bite my lips
To keep them inside
Nestling and bubbling
In the depths of my throat
To not blink fast
To not dry the tears
Before they roll down my cheek
Don't keep it inside
Don't deny it
There's no denying it anyway
You can't choose that easily
How and what to feel
So it is better
To let it out, scream it out
And what remains then
Nothing but peace

Watercolors

When I'm sad
The world is painted
In watercolors
I pour my tears
Into the paint
Of the world
And its colors
Become diluted
Everything pales
When confronted
With sadness
The only thing
That can make it
Vivid again
 Is love

Scars

My body
Aches from the battles
That rage on the inside
The invisible scars
All over my soul
Prevent me to let go
I realize they will
Never disappear
But I try to erase them
Not accepting that
By erasing my scars,
I am erasing myself too

All emotions

Sometimes
You need to
Let yourself feel
All the emotions
Inside you
Knowing that
One of them
Will be peace too

Breathe

The simplest action
Of inhaling and exhaling
Can sometimes
Heal your whole world
Bringing in love
And hope and peace
Pushing out fear
And pain and panic
Remember to breathe
When foes strike
Your beautiful mind
With a simple exhale
You will blow them away

Chaos

I often cannot
Deal with the Chaos
Inside my head
So I let it simply exist
Hoping that one day
It will go away
And if it persists
I remind myself that
In the dawn of time
Chaos was everywhere
And all the beauty
All the magic of the world
Came from that Chaos
So I hope that
Inside my head too
One day, there will be
Nothing but beauty
And magic

Bravery

Destiny has tried to destroy me
Beyond repair
So times so far
And every time
A scar remains
Etched deep in my skin
Yet somehow
I'm still standing
Willing to take on new adventures
Knowing they might
Cut me deeper than before
Is this what they call
Bravery

Healing

The process of healing
Isn't a one-step journey
But a long process
Of smaller
Every day decisions
To say yes
To things that feel good
And to say no
To things I no longer need

Finding my path

Finding my path
Through the unknown
Will always mean
Reaching deep down
And making a choice
Of light instead of dark

Keep my breath

Everytime I feel
Like I will drown
In the flood
Of my own feelings
I try to remember
I have drowned
So many times already
And survived
Because each flood
Taught me how
To keep my breath
For longer time

Return

People we love
Never really leave us
How could they
Matter cannot die
Atoms cannot
Be destroyed
They sometimes
Only have to evolve
Go back where
They came from:
The stars
So the next time
You look at the sky
And see that the
Stars are sparkling
Remember that
What you see
Are the souls of
People you love
Waving back
From their true home

Amulets

Love is the only thing
That can, even if only
Just for a second
Take away the fear of death
So people we love are
Amulets we use against
The encompassing fear
Of the inevitable
Because we know that
In a duel between
Love and Death
Love is the one who will
Always take victory

Lost in the mist

I would like to be lost
In the middle
Of a white warm mist
So that I could find
Way to myself again
Because I have lost it
Among the demands of life
Maybe falling on the ground
And being completely lost
Is what I need
To know who I am
Once again

Dream talk

Seeing you
Has become
A rare event in my life
We only ever see each other
In my dreams
We can only talk briefly
And most of the time
I don't even remember
Our words
I only remember
Just how much I miss you
And how grateful I am
That you once existed
In this world
So please
Whenever you can
Stop by in my dreams
Let's have a chat
A coffee like we used to have
Let's update each other
On what has been going on
I miss our conversations
More than anything
In those moments
When we talk in my dreams
You are less gone for me
Than ever

Sparkling darkness

When it feels like
Dark will swallow
Your whole being
Just remember
Even darkness
Sparkles sometimes
That's why stars
Come out every night
To remind us that
Beauty can be found
Even in the shadows
All we need to do
Is to look up to the sky

Happiness

Sometimes my body is
Overwhelmed by
This feeling of optimism
I feel like jumping out
Of my skin
But not because I cannot bear
Being inside my body
Anymore
Like I used to feel before
When sadness
Crushed it from all sides
But because my body
Has become the core
From which happiness
Radiates
Into the world

On the wings of the Moon

I have found myself again
On the wings of the Moon
When her beauty
Summoned particles
Of my daydreams
To come out once again
And spice my world
In the sweetest taste
Of inspiration

WANING CRESCENT MOON

Summer rain

Just like in the summer rain
I was drenched
In your love
In mere seconds
And I was unable
To dry my heart
From your kisses
Ever since

Petals

I don't know
The art of love that well
I have never given myself
This much to someone
Before
And I am constantly afraid
Of offering myself to you
Like the flowers open to the sun
Even though my insides
Ache for it
Can you still love me
Even though I am afraid
Can you still shine
So brightly
That my petals
Open without thinking

Speechless

They say

Love leaves you
Speechless
How is it then
That I was overwhelmed
By the flood of
The most beautiful words
Since I met you

Remembering

You told me one day
That we have spent
So many lives together already
And we kept finding each other
Across time and space
In that moment
It became clear to me
That the excitement
We felt the first time
We saw each other
Wasn't just butterflies
Of a new love being born
It was coming back home
Remembering
Recognizing
Each other's soul

Synchronised

Did you know
That our hearts
Synchronize
When we are
Close to each other
Even before we
Knew we were in love
Our bodies were
Aware of it
They synchronized
Our heartbeats
In perfect harmony
Hoping one day
We will realize it too

Chaotic Love

You walked straight
Into my head
Messing up the ties
Between my thoughts
And carried that mess
Into my soul
So I had no other choice
But to surrender myself
To the beautiful chaos
That is our love

Falling

Being with you means
Remaining eternally suspended
In that moment of falling
But forgetting completely
About the ground

Raindrops

I imagine rain
Are your fingertips
Sliding so sensuously
Along my spine
It makes me shiver
To think about
Its cold soft touch
It's just like your warm lips
Tracing all over my skin
You kiss me in the places
That I never knew existed
I am the thirsty ground
And your kisses
Are raindrops

The art of loving

The art of loving
Is a messy abstract piece
With thick layers of paint
And colors dripping
On each corner
If you do it right
Your hands are smeared
You have paint all over
Your face
But my-oh-my
Would you look at that
You have created
A miracle

Choreography

Night likes to dance
All over my skin
I allow it to touch me
Because it
Invites moonlight
To come out and play
Just like your lips
Invite mine
To unite in a new
Choreography

Give me

Give me your eyes so I can see the beauty
You found in my soul
Give me your hands so I can appreciate
All the curves of my body
Give me your lips so I can
Describe myself with loving words
Give me your body so I could realize
My existence is magic

Million suns

I love you
With all of my heart
With the strength
Of million suns
For me
You are starlight
Breaking the darkness
Of cold, cruel universe
Giving me hope
That there is something
Better than this
Something greater
Than all of us

Your presence

Your presence
Is like a melody
From my childhood
Well-known
Sang many times
Danced to
During numerous
Sleepless and
Restless nights
It wakes me up
From sadness
Invites me to dance
To the rhythm
Of our love

Plums

Your kisses taste
Like ripe summer plums
Warm from sun's
Loving caresses
Sweet from the dark
They were born in
Just like the stars

Understanding

That moment of perfect
Understanding
Is something I dreamed of
My entire life
So when we gaze deeply into
Each other's eyes
Or even exchange just a
Quick glance
A stolen moment among
A sea of people
I know the Universe had
A plan all along
And that all we did so far
In our lives
Was so we could live this one
Perfect moment

Complete and in shreds

I want you both
Complete and whole
And in pieces and shreds
I am not afraid
Of cutting myself
On your most perfect smile
So unleash it all
The love, the anger
The sadness, the trust
I can take it
I won't break

Looking at you

Looking at you is like looking at the horizon
I am the sky and you are the ground
Together and separated at the same time
Always filled with wild desire to touch

All around me

I feel you in the scent
Of a freshly cut grass
It reminds me of our
Evening walks in the sky
I spot you in the sparkle
Of a raindrop on the window
It makes me think about
Your eyes early in the morning
I notice you in the sound
Of birds singing at night
I remember how you laugh
When we dance around
I find you in myself
In every artery and vein
You race through them
Straight to my heart

Freckle me

Freckle me
With stardust and love
Bathe me in moonlight's
Loving hands
Let me become
One of the stars
So I would never leave
Your side

Limit

Can there really be a limit
Between two beings
Intertwined in their cores
Or is calling you "you"
And calling me "me"
Just a cut
In the middle of the whole

A moment

Rain is dipping lovingly
On a cold tin windowsill
Its tingling sounds
Like a clock ticking
Still, time is suspended
Enveloped in a storm
We lie, legs interlaced
Future or past are erased
There's only this moment
Only the next tick of the rain
Only you and me
Only our breaths intertwined

Morning coffee

Having a coffee with you
Especially the morning one
Means waking up in a pool
Of happiness and sunshine
When we exchange glances
Outraged by some new
Injustice in the world
We figure out that the
Solution to all the problems
Usually begins with an
"I love you"
So we start with that
Right there, with our coffees
Hoping the world will join

We exist in each other

We have existed in each other
Since the dawn of time
We have never really been apart
Because no atom can die
No particle can disappear
No matter can be destroyed
And we are built from the same ones

Thirst

This thirst for your soul
Controls my very existence
It made my soul come to be
So it would finally find yours

NEW MOON

Compassion

Why do I carry
So little love for myself
That I take and rip apart
My body in the mirror
I tear down everything I am
By comparing it
To other people
Why do I lack
That same compassion
That I pour out so freely
On other people

Bow down

I often let
Other people dictate
How I feel about myself
I surrender
Control over my body
And mind
To strangers who
Don't even know me
Well no more
I was made
Out of a lion's breath
To be ferocious
Strong
Untamed
Roaring my truth
Just like the wind
So I remind myself
Over and over again
It's the trees
Who bow down to the wind
Not the other way around

In spite of all odds

The world has tried to
Take away my gentleness
It wanted so badly
To make me stronger
By destroying every piece of me
That believes in fairytales
But no more
I will not let it
Take away my softness
It is my strongest trait
To be able to love
When everything around me
Screams in protest
And still I jump in
In spite of all odds
Hoping for the best
Now sweetie
That's true
Bravery

Underground rivers

My feelings run so deep
That even I am not
Aware of their strength
Don't mistake my calm
For composure
Or absence of feelings
Don't you know
That the underground rivers
Rage beneath us all the time
Just because
We never see them
Doesn't mean
They can't flood us
At any moment

Rivers of the wild

My bloodstream
Are rivers of the wild
Flowing together
Connected
In my heart
Carrying tempests
And winds and rains
Oh I need a storm
To feel whole again

Hurricane

You told me
I was a hurricane
And that you preferred
Smooth sailing
I am sorry
For all the destruction
I create
When I unleash
My true self
I want to learn
To let the ocean
Have its peace
But how can I sail smoothly
When my soul
Yearns to make wild love
To the waves

Promise

Love yourself
With all the fierceness
Of a lioness
Protecting its cubs
From predators

Reflection

Instead of begging
The mirror to
Describe my beauty
I will use beautiful words
As my reflection

Strong

Sometimes I feel
As strong
As a firefly
Embraced by darkness
Still willing to shine

Worship

My body is a temple
A place to worship
My soul

Unearth the stars

I look at my body
With a lover's eye
Like it is the place
Of pure pleasure
I touch my body
With a lover's hand
So that I can
Unearth the stars

Temple

My body is a temple
Where Universe resides
My cells are galaxies
And my atoms stars
So I enjoy my body
Praise it, adorn it
Because it is the place
Where my soul
Meets with the eternal
In every moment

Black Hole

My soul cannot be measured
By any adjective
Known to human language
Because it is infused
In the energy of the Universe
And it is just as inexplicable
As the shadows
Playing peek-a-boo
In the core of a black hole

Eclipse

I carry eclipse
In my heart
Like dark curtains
To protect people
From the strength
Of my Sun
Not realizing that
It is wildness
Of its warmth
That invites them in

Work of art

My body is unique
Made by life's skilful
Sculpting hands
My character is chiseled
Deep into the stone
Of my mind
Placed there by unknown forces
To complete the classical
Work of art
That is my soul

Magic

The odds of me becoming
Person that I am right now
Were millions to one
And still, somehow it happened
The Destiny must have cast
Endless spells
To invite my being to breathe
In this precise time and space
To be this person
And meet these people
Have this experience of life
I cannot think of a better proof
That our world is magic

Indomitable

I am as indomitable
As the moonlight
That flirty adventuress
Who reminds me
Every night
That I carry wild
Within

ACKNOWLEDGEMENT

I remember writing most of this book several years ago on my phone, in the breaks of writing my master thesis, while I lived alone abroad, away from my family and friends, with my thoughts and emotions so scrambled, that only writing them out helped make sense of my life. It was an emotional rollercoaster and one of the busiest times of my life, but also one of the most creative. Among other things, writing this book helped me deal with the trauma of losing a loved one, and the loneliness I felt at the time. However, it was with persistence, support and love from the people around me that this book truly came to be. So, my deepest gratitude goes to:

My Dad. Thank you for teaching me that life is an adventure and to always follow my guts. Those are the lessons I try to live by even today.

My Mom. Even though you are no longer here, I feel that I have found you again among these verses. Thank you for helping me live a creative life.

My husband. You brought me back to life in so many ways. Thank you for your endless support, love and for listening to my ramblings early in the morning or in the middle of the night.

My sister. Your wild love has taught me to love myself a little more and accept all those wild parts of myself. Thank you for all the support and involvement in the making of this book. Without you, none of this would have been possible.

My best friend. You were the first to read these words and my biggest supporter for years. Thank you for sticking with me no matter what, through my whole crazy healing journey.

All the friends and family members who supported me, read my poetry, listened to me talk about creativity and other crazy topics. You are the best people a person can wish for in their life and I couldn't be more grateful to be just lucky enough to have you in mine.

And finally, thank you, dear reader, for taking a chance with me. I hope you will let your wildness bloom and savor every second of it.

ABOUT THE AUTHOR

Anja J.

Anja is a creative soul who uses writing as a means to deal with emotions, thoughts and other demands of life. Through her very personal poetry, she talks about healing from trauma, grief, loss, as well as love and self-acceptance.

Follow her work online:
Instagram: @anjajauthor

Printed in Great Britain
by Amazon